DAEGEUM (HOW TO PLAY)

Mastering the Bamboo Flute: A Comprehensive Guide:Unlocking the Secrets of Traditional Korean music Performance

ETHA MOLINA

Table of Contents

CHAPTER ONE............................9

Background of the Daegeum
....9

Origins and Cultural Significance: 9

CHAPTER TWO........................15

Comprehending Musical Notation...................................15

Time and Rhythm...............15

CHAPTER THREE 21

Overcoming The Initial Challenges 21

Typical Errors Made by Novices 21

CHAPTER FOUR 27

Easy Scales and Activities .. 27

Simple Fingerings 27

CHAPTER FIVE 33

Examining Conventional Scores 33

How to Interpret Modern Sheet Music 33

CHAPTER SIX 39

Basics of Ensemble Playing 39

Growing in Intricacy of Music 39

CHAPTER SEVEN 45

Blending Conventional and Contemporary Designs 45

Developing a Unique Playing Style 45

CHAPTER EIGHT 51

Professional Repair and Tuning Services.......................51

Common Concerns and Detailed FAQs In this section:....................................51

Copyright 2024 Etha Molina

All rights reserved. Except for brief quotations included in critical reviews and certain other noncommercial uses allowed by copyright law, no part of this publication may be reproduced, distributed, or transmitted in any form or by any means, including photocopying, recording, or other electronic or mechanical methods, without the publisher's prior written permission.

Disclaimer: Etha Molina's personal knowledge and insight are the basis for this book's writing. The author has no connection to any organization, business, or person that is referenced in the book. The material offered should not be interpreted as professional advice; rather, it is only meant to be used for general informative reasons. Regarding specific concerns pertaining to playing an instrument, maintaining one, or any other topic addressed in this book, readers are urged to seek advice from qualified specialists or professionals. Any liability or responsibility for any loss or harm resulting from the use of the information provided herein is disclaimed by the author and publisher.

CHAPTER ONE
Background of the Daegeum

Origins and Cultural Significance: The Silla Dynasty (57 BC – 935 AD) is when the Daegeum, a traditional Korean bamboo flute, first appeared. It is highly regarded for its warm, rich tone and is frequently connected to shamanic ceremonies and Korean royal music, signifying harmony and serenity.

The Daegeum is an instrument that has developed over ages from a basic bamboo pipe to a complex device with intricate finger holes and a buzzing membrane that enhances its tone and enables more emotive performances.

Famous Daegeum Players: The instrument's popularity has been greatly aided by well-known Daegeum masters like Hwang Byung-ki and Jeong Seung-hyeon, who have demonstrated the instrument's depth and adaptability in both traditional and modern works.

Function in Traditional Korean Music: The Daegeum plays a crucial role in genres such as Nongak (farmer's music), Sanjo (instrumental solo), and Gukak (court music), adding a unique melodic voice to the moving narrative.

Influence on Modern Music: By fusing the Daegeum's traditional sound with cutting-edge approaches, current musicians have incorporated it into a variety of genres, including jazz and world music, to provide unique, cross-cultural musical experiences.

Comprehending the Daegeum

The daegeum is a traditional bamboo flute from Korea that is well-known for its unique sound and rich, deep tones. Its distinctive tone is produced by the vibration of a membrane hole (Cheong) in the huge main tube. In order to alter the pitch, players blow across the mouthpiece and cover the finger holes. The fundamental scales and melodies should be mastered by beginners by practicing correct breath control and finger placement.

The Daegeum's portions

The mouthpiece (ipgung), the main body (cheonggyeong), the finger holes (kkwaenggari), and the membrane hole (cheonggong) are the main components that make up the daegeum. Each component is essential to the creation of sound. Gaining an understanding of these elements facilitates the learning process for novices by teaching them the correct techniques for holding, tuning, and playing the instrument.

Kinds and Differences

The daegeum comes in various forms; the jeong-ak daegeum is used for classical music, and the sanjo daegeum is used for folk music. Each kind is suited to a certain musical genre and varies somewhat in size and tuning. The regular Jeong-ak daegeum is a better place for beginners to start because it is more frequently used and adaptable, making it easier to get guidance and instructional materials.

Sound Properties

The daegeum creates a distinctive, resonant sound that is distinguished by the membrane's faint buzzing and its deep, gentle tones. This sound is produced by carefully manipulating breath and finger movements. In order to properly enjoy and imitate the instrument's rich acoustic features, beginners should concentrate on creating a consistent embouchure and playing lengthy tones.

The Significance Of Korean Ensembles

In traditional Korean music groups, the daegeum is an essential instrument that frequently leads songs and provides harmonic support.

Folk tunes, court music, and contemporary compositions frequently use it. Beginners can better grasp the cultural value of ensemble pieces and improve their overall musicianship and performance skills by practicing ensemble pieces with the support of an understanding of their function within the group.

Selecting the Best Daegeum for Novices

Beginners should choose a Daegeum that is carefully made and the right size for comfortable handling. Important considerations are bamboo quality, craftsmanship, and tuning precision. It's a good idea to ask more seasoned players or instructors for advice, and you might choose to start with a student model, which is usually less expensive and ideal for learning the fundamentals.

Comprehending Musical Notation

Learn the seven fundamental sounds (A, B, C, D, E, F, and G) in order to begin comprehending musical notation. Pitch representations of each note serve as the fundamental units of music. To become acquainted with the pitches of these notes, practice recognizing them on a musical staff and pay attention to their sounds. To ensure that the notes match precisely, use a keyboard or tuner.

CHAPTER TWO

Comprehending Musical Notation

Understanding the symbols and notations used to represent various musical elements is necessary in order to read sheet music. Learn the staff first. It has five lines and four spaces, each of which represents a different note. Get acquainted with note locations and the treble clef. Start by reading easy Daegeum compositions, then work your way up to more difficult ones.

Time and Rhythm

In music, timing and rhythm are essential. They choose the notes' length and structure. To begin, become familiar with the whole, half, quarter, eighth, and sixteenth note values. Practice maintaining a steady beat and clapping out various beats with a metronome. To guarantee precise time, gradually incorporate these rhythms into your Daegeum practice.

The Modes and Scales in Daegeum Music

The basis of melodies in Daegeum music is made up of scales and modes. Start by playing the fundamental major and minor scales one note at a time. Proceed to investigate conventional Korean modes, such as the pentatonic scale, which is frequently employed in Daegeum music. Regular practice of these scales can help you build muscle memory and enhance your ability to perform a variety of melodies.

Simple Terminologies in Music

Learn some basic terminology used in music so that you can comprehend sheet music and instructions more easily. It's important to understand concepts like dynamics (volume), articulation (note-playing technique), and tempo (musical pace). Find out what they mean and how they relate to your playing. For instance, practice using a metronome to adjust the tempo and adjust the dynamics by playing notes softly or loudly.

Opening and Putting Together Your Daegeum

Start by carefully unpacking the daegeum and making sure the mouthpiece, tuning slide, and main body are all there. Put the mouthpiece firmly on the body and turn the tuning slide to the neutral position to assemble. Avoid using any force on the daegeum as this could harm the fragile bamboo.

Easy-to-Start Exercises

In order to develop your skills, start with basic exercises. To improve breath control, practice holding a long tone for several seconds at a time.

Appropriate Upkeep and Care

Your daegeum remains in excellent shape with regular care. Clean the interior with a soft cloth or swab to get rid of any moisture after each session. To prevent warping, keep the instrument in a dry place and frequently inspect it for damage or cracks. To preserve the bamboo, lightly coat it with natural oil.

First Audio Production

Starting with the daegeum horizontally on the mouthpiece, develop a comfortable "O" shape with your lips. Gently release the breath, modifying your embouchure until a distinct, clear note emerges. Breathe steadily and evenly while practicing, paying attention to the pitch and airflow.

After that, start with simple scales and play them slowly at first, then faster and faster as you get more comfortable. Aim for precise finger placement and seamless note-to-note transitions.

Organizing a Practice Area

Make a relaxing, distraction-free practicing space. Ascertain enough illumination and a posture-supporting chair. Maintain easy access to your metronome, sheet music, and other equipment. Set aside this area just for practice in order to create a habit and increase your learning effectiveness.

Tips for Handling and Taking Care of

After every usage, wipe down your Daegeum with a gentle towel to eliminate any remaining moisture or debris for optimal maintenance. Keep it in a cool, dry place, preferably in a case to keep dust and physical harm off of it.

The Daegeum should not be exposed to extremely high or low humidity levels as this may cause the bamboo to split. To keep the bamboo from drying out, lightly oil it from time to time. Also, make sure the mouthpiece is constantly clean for a clear, resonant sound.

CHAPTER THREE
Overcoming The Initial Challenges

One of the most frequent difficulties when learning the Daegeum is maintaining a clear, steady tone. Try blowing over the mouthpiece while holding the instrument against your lips to practice your embouchure. Experiment with different angles until you reach the sweet spot where the sound is clear. To improve your consistency and breath control, start with long, sustained notes. To guarantee precise note production and seamless transitions, practice placing your fingers on the holes on a regular basis.

Typical Errors Made by Novices

A common mistake made by novices is to grip the Daegeum too tightly, which can deteriorate sound quality and wear out their hands.

Try holding the instrument with your hands and fingers relaxed, making sure your grip is firm enough to maintain control without putting too much strain on your muscles.

Breath management is another typical error to make; concentrate on steady, regulated breathing instead of shoving air through the instrument. In order to establish a solid foundation, practice carefully and methodically rather than speeding through scales and exercises.

Monitoring Progress

Establish measurable objectives for yourself, like as learning a basic tune or mastering a specific scale, so you can monitor your progress.

To evaluate your progress objectively, record your performance at regular intervals to evaluate your tone, rhythm, and finger dexterity. Maintain a practice notebook where you record your tasks, difficulties, and successes. This will keep you inspired and give you a detailed history of your progress over time.

Responses to Commonly Asked Questions

Beginners frequently wonder, "How do I produce a clear tone?" pay attention to your embouchure and breath control. Start with fundamental scales, extended tones, and straightforward melodies when answering the question, "What should I practice daily?" "How do **I read traditional Korean music notation?"** You start by becoming familiar with the fundamentals of Jeongganbo, the notation system used in Korea, which employs a grid to represent rhythm and pitch. Regarding maintenance, to maintain your Daegeum in top shape, clean and oil it on a regular basis.

Appropriate Balance and Posture

Make sure your weight is spread properly when you stand with your feet shoulder-width apart. Maintain a straight back and relaxed shoulders. Playing the Daegeum in this stance gives you a solid base, which improves control and sound quality.

Placing Your Hands on the Daegeum

Grasp the Daegeum with your right hand stabilizing the bottom and your left hand close to the top. The pads of your fingers should rest on the perforations, forming a natural curve. This arrangement enables fluid note transitions and accurate finger movements.

Methods of Breathing

Breathe deeply through your nose, pushing your chest out from behind your diaphragm. Consistently exhale into the Daegeum while controlling the airflow with your abdominal muscles. To produce a clear and sustained tone, breathing must be controlled and consistent.

Steer clear of strain and injury

While playing, keep your hands and fingers loose and try not to tense up too much. To avoid tension, make sure to extend your fingers and wrists before and after practice. During practice sessions, taking pauses can also assist lower the chance of injury.

Executing Posture Manoeuvres

Include posture exercises in your practice regimen. For example, stand up against a wall to maintain a straight back. To increase your coordination and general stability, practice one-footed balance. These drills improve your playing technique and help you maintain proper posture.

Making the First Sound

Holding the daegeum horizontally and placing your lips on the mouthpiece will cause it to make the initial sound. Make sure your lips are firm but relaxed as you gently press them on the embouchure opening. Like blowing through a bottle top, blow a continuous stream of air through the hole and move your lips until you hear a distinct tone. To achieve a steady tone, practice this repeatedly.

CHAPTER FOUR
Easy Scales and Activities

To familiarize oneself with the range of the daegeum, start with basic scales.

To begin, play the fundamental C major scale, gradually rising and falling, and making sure that every note is distinct and in tune. Include exercises that emphasize making seamless transitions between notes, like repeatedly playing brief sequences of three to five notes. Finger coordination is enhanced and muscle memory is developed through this practice.

Simple Fingerings

The first step in learning basic Daegeum fingerings is figuring out which holes to cover for each note. Starting with the basic fingerings for the first octave, cover and reveal the holes with your index, middle, and ring fingers. To produce proper pitches, practice playing each note in the correct order while paying attention to the positioning and pressure of your fingers. As you get more familiar with the fundamentals, gradually advance to more intricate fingerings.

Managing Tone and Volume

Learning to control your breath and make necessary embouchure adjustments is necessary to control tone and volume on the Daegeum. Breathe lightly and employ a relaxed embouchure for softer tones. Firm up your embouchure and raise your air pressure to produce louder, more forceful tones. Try a variety of lip positions and breath pressures to determine the best combination for getting the right volume and tone.

Building Up Your Embouchure Strength

To produce a sound that is clear and steady, you must strengthen your embouchure. To practice long tones, try holding a single note at a constant pitch and loudness for as long as you can. Include lip-flexibility exercises, like alternating between notes with different finger locations for higher and lower pitches. Your lips and facial muscles will develop the requisite strength and endurance with regular practice of these workouts.

Decorative elements and embellishments

Pay attention to grace notes, trills, and slides when you're playing Daegeum to add ornamentation and flourishes. Practice grace notes first. These are brief notes that are played just before the main note. Slides call for a fluid transition between pitches, while trills need quick switching between two neighboring notes. To ensure accuracy, start out gently and pick up pace gradually. Use these methods to develop control and muscle memory in scales and easy songs.

Dynamics and Vibrato

In order to produce a quivering impression when playing a note on the Daegeum, you must oscillate your breath. Play a steady note at first, then gradually pulse your breath while adjusting the pace and intensity. Practice changing your breath pressure to play notes loudly (forte) and softly (piano) to achieve different dynamics. To practice these skills, use extended tones and scales, being careful to keep the same tone quality throughout.

Using Expression and Emotion in Play

Consider interpreting the mood and character of the music in order to play the Daegeum with emotion and expression.

To portray a variety of emotions, play around with articulation, dynamics, and tempo. For instance, during gloomy portions, employ slower tempos and softer dynamics; during exuberant moments, utilize faster tempos and more aggressive playing. To progressively build your own style, practice expressive playing by listening to recordings made by professionals and imitating their subtleties.

More Complex Fingerings

On the Daegeum, advanced fingerings entail utilizing different finger positions to produce more intricate passages and seamless transitions. To become comfortable with the positioning of these alternate fingerings, study finger charts and practice scales.

Play etudes and works that call for rapid note changes to incorporate advanced fingerings into your daily practice while maintaining accuracy and fluidity.

Applying Methods in Real Practice

If you want to successfully add advanced methods to your Daegeum practice, set up a program that allows a certain time for each ability. Warm-up exercises that emphasize finger flexibility and breath control should come first. After that, set some time to practice expression, dynamics, vibrato, and ornamentation. To maintain steady timing, use a metronome. Then, progressively include these approaches into your repertoire, concentrating on one area at a time to prevent overload.

Comprehending Korean Musical Notation

Learn the meanings of the conventional symbols before attempting to understand Korean musical notation for the Daegeum. Korean notation uses a grid system, with each box representing a rhythmic unit. It is frequently based on Jeongganbo. Acquire knowledge of the basic rhythmic patterns and note placement within these boxes. To increase your confidence, practice finding and playing with short notated sentences.

CHAPTER FIVE

Examining Conventional Scores

Scores of traditional Korean music for the Daegeum frequently have extensive notations for rhythm, tone, and particular playing styles. Start with easier work, paying attention to the main melody and rhythmic patterns. Take note of the distinct markings for breath control and fingering. Move up to increasingly complicated scores gradually as you gain familiarity with the conventional notation style.

How to Interpret Modern Sheet Music

Western notation or a combination of Western and traditional symbols may be used in modern sheet music for the Daegeum. Learn the fundamental staff, clefs, and time signatures first. Pay close attention to how Western notes translate to their Daegeum counterparts, noting any unusual performance strategies that may be mentioned. To help you connect your grasp of both notation systems, practice with some basic modern works.

Exercises for Practice with Notation

Practice Daegeum notation on a daily basis to improve your reading and playing skills. Start with basic rhythmic patterns and scales written in both traditional and modern notation. Gradually add modifications and ornamentations to make the work more intricate. Make use of these drills to sharpen your sight-reading abilities and cultivate a more intuitive understanding of the notation.

Making the Switch from Simple to Complicated Pieces

Making the move from simple to sophisticated Daegeum pieces is needed for planning. Start with easy melodies and work your way up to more complex rhythms and approaches. Divide difficult elements into smaller, more manageable chunks, and practice each one gradually before putting them together. You can easily master advanced compositions with consistent practice and small challenges.

Well-known Songs for Beginners

Start with easy, well-known songs like "Mary Had a Little Lamb" and "Twinkle, Twinkle, Little Star" to become accustomed to the Daegeum's breath control and finger placements. These songs are great for beginners to practice and learn basic techniques because they usually feature simple notes and repeating patterns.

Dissecting Songs

To dissect a melody, first determine which notes make up the melody and practice each note alone. To make sure every note is played accurately, use a tuner. After you're at ease with the notes, work on effortlessly connecting them while paying attention to your finger movements and breathing steadily.

Increasing Pitch Precision

It takes regular practice with a tuner and concentration on breath control to increase pitch accuracy. Make sure your lips are shaped correctly (embouchure), and practice holding extended tones on each note to help build fine pitch control and muscle memory. It can also be beneficial to record yourself and compare it with a reference pitch.

Combining Different Melody Techniques

It takes seamless integration of breath control, finger placements, and embouchure modifications to combine techniques in melodies.

To start, practice scales to improve your respiratory control and fluid finger movements. Next, use similar methods on basic melodies, making sure that every note is audible and that the transitions are seamless.

Compiling a List of Songs

Choosing a range of easy songs to practice on a daily basis is the first step in developing a repertoire. Start with simple tunes and work your way up to more intricate ones as your abilities grow. Your Daegeum playing will become more versatile and confident with regular practice and song selection.

Overview of Conventional Works

Start with easy tunes like "Arirang" when learning traditional Korean music for the Daegeum. Concentrate on achieving the traditional tone by honing your slow, deliberate breathing and fluid finger movements. To become acquainted with the melody and rhythm, practice with sheet music and recordings. Then, try to imitate the delicate details and embellishments that are typical of traditional Korean music.

Having Company When Playing

To gain a sense of the timing and dynamics of playing with accompaniment, start with a basic composition and practice using a recording of the accompaniment. To guarantee that you stay on time with the accompaniment, pay special attention to your rhythm and tone. Gradually transition to in-person practice sessions with a pianist or other musician, emphasizing harmony maintenance and sound merging throughout the composition.

CHAPTER SIX

Basics of Ensemble Playing

Prior to practicing with the group for ensemble playing, make sure you have a solid understanding of your role. To maintain coherence, count rests and cues and pay close attention to other areas.

To produce a cohesive performance during rehearsals, concentrate on speaking clearly with other players and controlling your volume in relation to the group.

Growing in Intricacy of Music

Start using more complicated musical elements like vibrato, dynamic contrasts, and quicker parts to make your music more complex.

Divide challenging passages into smaller, more manageable chunks, then practice them slowly before progressively picking up the pace.

Develop your finger agility and control by practicing scales and arpeggios on a regular basis.

This will empower you to confidently take on increasingly complex work.

Getting Ready for an Intermediate Performance

Choose pieces for your intermediate performance that will test your abilities while remaining inside your comfort zone. Establish a practice plan to handle any technological issues and guarantee that every component is flawless.

Gain confidence by practicing in front of friends and family. Pay attention to your stage presence, including proper posture and audience interaction, to produce a captivating presentation.

Learning the Key Daegeum Pieces

To fully understand the subtleties and emotions included in the music, begin by listening to recordings of the classic Daegeum compositions. Divide the piece into doable chunks and practice each one gradually, paying attention to breath control and finger placement. Increase your speed gradually as you get more at ease. Take note of customary embellishments and make an effort to replicate them precisely. You can monitor your progress and find areas for development by routinely recording your practice sessions.

Techniques for Solo Performance

A solo Daegeum performance calls for both technical mastery and expressive emotional range. Play scales and arpeggios to develop your breath control and finger dexterity. Put your attention on phrasing and dramatic contrasts to give your performance more emotional depth.

So that you can concentrate on expression rather than reading the music, make sure you fully memorize your parts. To overcome stage fear and increase confidence, mentally picture the performance.

Expert Group Performance

Accomplishment in an ensemble requires excellent listening skills and accurate timing. Practice with a metronome to ensure you maintain a steady rhythm.Observe the dynamics and other musicians' cues carefully.

Develop the ability to blend your sound with the group by adjusting your volume and tone as needed. Regular rehearsals are crucial for synchronizing your parts and refining the overall performance. Effective communication with your ensemble members will enhance the cohesiveness of the group.

Customizing Interpretations

Personalizing your interpretations of Daegeum music involves understanding the historical and cultural context of each piece. Experiment with different tempos, dynamics, and phrasing to find a style that resonates with you. Incorporate your unique emotional expressions while staying true to the piece's traditional elements. Listen to various interpretations by other musicians for inspiration. Keep a practice journal to note your creative ideas and reflections on each piece.

Performance Preparation Tips

Preparing for a Daegeum performance involves more than just practicing the music. Ensure your instrument is in top condition by checking for any issues and tuning it properly. Warm up thoroughly to avoid strain and enhance your performance quality.

Plan your practice sessions to cover difficult sections and perform full run-throughs. Visualize your performance, including your stage presence and audience interaction. Lastly, manage pre-performance nerves with relaxation techniques like deep breathing or meditation. Basics of Musical Improvisation

To begin improvising on the Daegeum, start by familiarizing yourself with the fundamental scales and modes used in Korean music. Practice playing simple phrases within these scales, experimenting with different note combinations and rhythms. Focus on listening to traditional Daegeum music to understand the stylistic nuances, then try to mimic and expand upon these patterns in your own practice sessions.

Creating Original Melodies

Creating original melodies on the Daegeum involves combining your understanding of scales with your creative instincts. Begin by selecting a scale and playing it slowly, allowing your mind to wander and experiment with different sequences of notes. Aim for expressive phrasing and try to evoke emotions through your playing. Record your practice sessions to capture spontaneous ideas and refine them into more structured melodies over time.

CHAPTER SEVEN
Blending Conventional and Contemporary Designs

Blending traditional and modern styles in the Daegeum requires a deep appreciation of both. Start by mastering traditional pieces to understand the core techniques and expressions. Then, listen to modern music across various genres and identify elements that could complement the Daegeum's sound. Experiment with incorporating contemporary rhythms, harmonies, and effects into your playing, creating a fusion that respects tradition while exploring new musical landscapes.

Developing a Unique Playing Style

Developing a unique playing style on the Daegeum involves a combination of technical proficiency and personal expression. Focus on perfecting your breath control, finger techniques, and articulation. Simultaneously, reflect on what inspires you musically and integrate those influences into your practice. Over time, your personal preferences and interpretations will naturally shape a distinctive style that reflects your musical identity.

Improvisation Exercises

To enhance your improvisation skills on the Daegeum, engage in specific exercises that challenge your creativity and technical ability. One effective exercise is to choose a simple melody and improvise variations on it, altering the rhythm, dynamics, and articulation. Another exercise is to play along with a backing track or a metronome, focusing on maintaining a steady rhythm while exploring different melodic ideas. Regularly practicing these exercises will build confidence and fluency in your improvisation.

Preparing for Public Performances: Before stepping on stage, thorough preparation is key. This includes rehearsing repertoire until it's second nature, ensuring all equipment is in optimal condition, and organizing logistics like travel and timing. Rehearsing in different settings can simulate the live experience, helping to anticipate and mitigate potential issues.

Stage Presence and Confidence: Develop a commanding presence on stage by maintaining good posture and projecting confidence through body language. Practice eye contact with the audience to establish a connection and convey emotion. Utilize the space effectively, moving with purpose and energy that matches the music's mood.

Engaging with the Audience: Connect with your audience by acknowledging their presence with a smile or greeting. During breaks or transitions, share brief insights about the music or instruments to build rapport. Adjust performance dynamics based on audience response, keeping them engaged throughout the show.

Managing Performance Anxiety: Combat nerves with effective techniques such as controlled breathing, visualization of successful past performances, and positive self-talk. Practicing mindfulness or meditation before performances can help center your focus and reduce anxiety. Channel nervous energy into expressive playing or movement on stage.

Post-Performance Evaluation: Reflect on your performance to identify strengths and areas for improvement. Consider feedback from peers or mentors objectively to refine future performances. Assess technical aspects like sound quality and timing, as well as audience interaction and overall emotional impact. Use this evaluation to inform your practice and preparation for future live performances.

Cleaning and Storing Your Daegeum: To keep your Daegeum in optimal condition, regularly clean it after each use. Use a soft, lint-free cloth to wipe down the exterior and interior surfaces, removing moisture and debris. Avoid using harsh chemicals or excessive water to prevent damage to the bamboo. Store your Daegeum in a dry, cool place away from direct sunlight and humidity, ideally enclosed in a protective cover or case to guard against dust buildup and unintentional damage.

Routine Maintenance Practices: Incorporate simple routine maintenance into your playing schedule to ensure your Daegeum performs well over time. Check for any loose joints or cracks by gently tapping the instrument and listening for changes in tone or rattling sounds. Keep the bamboo moisturized by occasionally applying a small amount of almond or walnut oil to maintain its natural flexibility and prevent drying out, especially in dry climates.

Identifying and Fixing Common Issues: Learn to recognize and address common issues that may arise with your Daegeum. Inspect the joints and bindings for signs of wear or separation. If you notice buzzing or inconsistent tones, check the bamboo for cracks or loose bindings that may need to be re-tied or glued. For stuck or sluggish keys, carefully clean around the holes and joints with a soft brush or cloth to remove any debris that could be obstructing movement.

Extending the Instrument's Lifespan: To extend the lifespan of your Daegeum, practice careful handling and storage habits. Avoid exposing it to extreme temperatures or sudden changes in humidity, as these can cause the bamboo to warp or crack. Regularly inspect and maintain the instrument to catch minor issues before they escalate, ensuring that it continues to produce clear and vibrant tones over the years.

CHAPTER EIGHT
Professional Repair and Tuning Services

When in doubt or facing more complex issues, seek assistance from a qualified instrument technician experienced with traditional Korean flutes like the Daegeum. Professional services can include re-tying joints, repairing cracks, or adjusting tuning to maintain the instrument's optimal performance and resonance. Establishing a relationship with a trusted technician ensures that your Daegeum receives expert care when needed, preserving its quality and value for future generations.

Common Concerns and Detailed FAQs

In this section: you'll find answers to common questions beginners have about playing the Daegeum. From understanding its traditional significance to practical queries about maintenance and tuning, this segment addresses everything you need to know to start your journey with confidence.

Addressing Physical Discomfort while Playing
Playing the Daegeum requires proper posture and breath control.

This section provides practical tips on how to sit or stand comfortably, ensuring your body remains relaxed and aligned. Techniques for stretching and warming up before practice sessions are also covered to prevent strain and enhance your playing experience.

Balancing Practice with Other Commitments
Learning the Daegeum is rewarding but requires consistent practice. Here, you'll discover effective strategies for managing your practice time alongside work, school, or other responsibilities. From setting realistic goals to creating a structured practice schedule, these tips help you maximize your progress without overwhelming your daily life.

Financial Considerations in Playing the Daegeum Owning and maintaining a Daegeum involves certain costs. This segment outlines essential financial considerations, such as instrument purchase or rental options, maintenance expenses, and potential costs associated with lessons or workshops. It provides insights into budgeting effectively while pursuing your passion for the Daegeum.

Tips for Staying Motivated Staying motivated in your Daegeum journey is crucial for long-term progress. This section offers practical advice on setting achievable milestones, finding inspiration from the music you love, and connecting with fellow players or mentors. Techniques for overcoming plateaus and celebrating small victories keep your enthusiasm high as you develop your skills.

In conclusion, mastering the Daegeum is a journey that intertwines discipline, creativity, and cultural appreciation. Throughout this guide, we have explored the fundamentals of playing this traditional Korean instrument, from understanding its construction and tuning to mastering essential techniques such as tonguing and vibrato.

Beyond technique, learning the Daegeum is a gateway to understanding Korean music's rich tapestry and its role in cultural expression. Each note played resonates not just with sound but with centuries of tradition and emotion. As you progress, remember that perfection is not the goal; rather, it's the connection you forge with the instrument and its heritage that truly matters.

To excel, consistency in practice is key. The daegeum rewards dedication with its unique sound and versatility, whether in solo performances or as part of traditional ensembles.

Embrace challenges as opportunities to grow, and celebrate every milestone achieved along the way.

Moreover, as you delve deeper into the Daegeum's repertoire, explore its potential in contemporary contexts and collaborations. The blending of tradition with innovation ensures its relevance in today's musical landscape, offering limitless avenues for exploration and personal expression.

Finally, share your journey with others. Whether teaching, performing or simply sharing the beauty of the Daegeum's melodies, your passion can inspire future generations to embrace this instrument and its cultural significance.

In closing, the Daegeum is not merely an instrument but a storyteller of Korea's musical heritage. As you continue to play, may each note resonate with reverence for tradition, creativity, and the joy of musical discovery.

Made in the USA
Monee, IL
25 February 2025